That Settles It

A Journey of Spiritual Poetry

Anthony C. Settles

ISBN 979-8-88616-075-8 (paperback)
ISBN 979-8-88616-076-5 (digital)

Christian Faith Publishing
832 Park Avenue
Meadville, PA 16335
www.christianfaithpublishing.com

Printed in the United States of America

Contents

Introduction

Freely, Freely You Have Received; Freely, Freely Give

Poetry (I believe) has been a part of me since before I can remember, though I never started writing until seventh grade. Jesus has been Lord of my life since age twenty-three and has since been a catalyst to my mind, helping change the flow of gift in me to speak more clearly of Him. While cleansing me with His presence, He is and always will be unchanged at my relationship to Him. I am so thankful!

I've been allowed many experiences in my walk, which have brought me the blessings of an obedient heart, and the chastening of the Lord when needed—too often, I must confess. Through it all, at the age of sixty-one, I can say I have learned that His grace is sufficient for my many inefficiencies, and the freedom of that understanding blesses me to write without fear of the One I love!

Paula, my wife and God-send, works diligently at typing my chicken scratch. Her mom, whom I call my mom, encourages me and is an incredible spellchecker; and sister Lin, you are a blessing!

Be blessed as you read *That Settles It*!

And thank you!

About My Logo

One night, years ago,
while working in a rescue mission,
I could not go to sleep.
Out of the blue,
a tic-tac-toe bounced
into my mind
and refused to go away.
I got out of bed,
grabbed my pencil and paper,
prayed for help, and in a
few minutes had my logo.

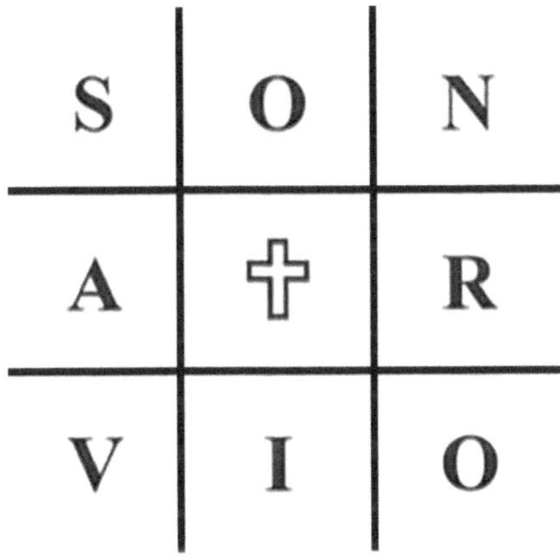

That Settles It

Long before my birth
to this world,
Long before I was attached
to my name,
There was a name attached
to the Three-Equals-One.
Holy, holy, holy are they!
His ways are higher than
my thoughts, His thoughts
chose me free will.
Sin was my name to the
Father's eyes
Who saw my natural birth.
That name took flight
to Christ on the Cross
changing my name at the
cost of His worth.
Worthy is the Name
of Jesus.
Long before my birth
to this world,
Long before I was attached
to my name,

There was a plan to fill
my soul at the choosing
of His name
to trump the name
from Adam's sin.
I've carried with
all of its shame
to the trumpets
proclaim.
Glory, glory, glory!
The Holy Spirit
came to change
my name!
Written in the
Lamb's Book of Life
and the devil be damned.
That settles it!
Hallelujah!

October 24, 2018

Not One Sparrow

From out of the sky
comes spiraling down
a fluttering sparrow to the ground.

God's all-seeing eye
comes focus to meet
this unique creature
as its heart stopped to beat.

Apart from God, no sparrow falls.
His love for them has no flaws.
If all the sparrows in the world
banded together in a whirl
and danced before the Lord of Host,
His pleasure would be utter most.

Yet small compared to His joy
at saving either girl or boy,
If life for you seems spiraling down
destined to the cold hard ground.

Here is wisdom you can borrow:
He loves you more than all the sparrows.

Beckoning Hands of the Carpenter

Come to the Hands where truth is found,
come to His beckoning Hands.
Bring with you the weight of sin
to His Hands and lay it down.
Have you troubles? Don't despair!
Strong Hands, tho' gentle, truly care.
Once placed in them you'll understand
the power of His Hands.

Carpenter's hands work marvelous plans
from the blueprints laid before them,
beaten and worn, tho' strong through the wear,
hands of a carpenter build and repair.
Beckoning Hands created the world
of planets, love, and life.
Harmony was foundation
to the frame so void of strife.

Come! Called the Carpenter to the two,
as life He hammered in them.
Let's dance the dance of workmanship
for my Hands have soundly made you.
Called back did they from homes of clay,
for dust was formed about them.
From these temples we're in place,
we'll dance with you the dance of grace
for Your Hands have soundly made us.

And dance they did in the Carpenter's Hands,
dancing to the builder's plans.
In love with every breath they drew,
unhindered by a knowledge true;
Free will was carved within them.

Fallen angel, lying blur, pons to be the Carpenter.
Knew the truth of house design
and peeked inside the window blind
in hopes to tear the house down.

Hath He said, is it so,
The Carpenter must surely know.
You'll be as wise as He is.

Come now, come now take a bite!
Do it to it, do it right!
Thus, they did and thus the night
of dancing in the darkness.

From the Carpenter's Hands, the Carpenter came
to repair the damage done to the frame
for the foundation stayed the same,
His Hands had firmly laid it.

Beckoning Hands of the Carpenter
were nailed to a wooden frame.
Ironic is the truth of it
our houses are to blame!
Yet hear a story, listen well
Oh, houses where you live,
from dust to dust, the house will go.
Where then is the soul to live?

Beckoning Hands of the Carpenter,
Call, come, and dance again.
I'm building you a second home
where liars can't peek in.
For love of You, I dance the death
nailed upon a tree.
An ugly death my Hands designed
to set my buildings free!
Yes, friend, workmanship is never free—
I paid the labor's cost.

My Carpenter's Hands are beckoning
now
Come now—be repaired at my Cross

2006

Wardrobe = Tree of Shame

No longer clothed in righteousness
Having eaten from forbidden fruit
Their new wardrobe called shameful guilt
Led Him to a tree of shame for our guilt.

What a shame, so few share it!

August 9, 2016

Change Comes Hard

Change comes hard,
especially to a
self-confessed dinosaur
like myself.
But it is so nice
to have such a
wonderful place called
the Lowcountry
while fighting the battle
of change.

White Stag

Poem:
White stag paws the air while sniffing the wind;
senses the scent of the hunter men.
Hound on his heel, he bolts away, lightning fast
in the cool of autumn day.
Across the meadow, but a flash, through the wood
a graceful dash—"the hound bays to the hunter."

Song:
Can you feel the pounding coming from the deer
Burning heartbeat drumming out of fear?
What will become of the deer?
Glide away, white stag.
Leap through the woods,
Jump all the fences, for life is too good
to let the dog trap you for the hunters to shoot.
Glide away, white stag, till you come to the brook—
Till you come to the brook.

Poem:
Behind the hounds ride hunters on horse, screaming cries
of hunter discourses; gun-toting hunters with one common mind,
sport for food and tan the hide of the stag they're in pursuit of.
Life is a peril the stag knows well as hours fly by with the
hunt on the trail; life seems sure to find and end, as energy seeps
from the blood within, "White stag on the verge of quitting."

Back to the song piece:

Poem:
Help comes carried by the breeze, smell the brook, taste the tease.
Forget the danger close behind, life's in front its heart
to find; and the stag has hope rekindled.
To the brook, a bounding leap! In its midst of sweet relief
Lost is his scent to the hound on his heels.
The hunters have lost their could-have-been meal.
White stag drinks the drink of his life
Then lies to rest on the other side of the brook—
"his friend and his safety."

Song:
Can you feel the heartbeat coming from the deer
Drumming peaceful beats now void of fear?
Look what's become of the deer.
Glide away, white stag, leap while you dream.
You've jumped all the fences and found the good stream.
The dog is forgotten, the hunters are gone.
Glide on, white stag, you've come to the brook—
You've come to the brook.

White stags are all who've been washed in the blood,
Yearning for more of our Savior's love, safety, comfort, and
Strength for the race; floods the soul while setting the pace,
filling our hearts to long for our Lord,
As white stag for the brooks giving water.

Walk While You Work

Is your concern
that the building is full
come Sunday morning chimes,
more than the love that
the temple be full
where the soul resides;
And if so, what will you do
when he comes for you,
the devil and his temptations!
Run back quick if you've
lost your first love,
to walking in the love from above
so that they can once again
be anointed for your blessings of
your walk while you work.

Read Revelation 1:12–13, then 2:1–7

January 1, 2018

Empathy Rekindled

Unlike us, You're never one to turn to dust
With aging bones that seem to fill full of rust
on cold, damp days reminding us
who You are and who we're not

You sent Your Son, so unlike us
to take on form of simple dust
to work God's plan with
bones capable to feel the aging rust
that makes You oh so like us!
Jesus so like us

Spirit moves within the flock,
Shepherd's staff points to the Rock
Sheep graze in and out of time
as the watch sets to unwind
hands held in His forever

Becoming so like You!
In Christ!

Hallelujah!

A Conversation with Jesus

Jesus,
You're not willing that any should perish,
Yet we know that many will.
How is it that salvationship
Seems so hard to fill?

*"The world's will has long
been for self."*

Yes, Lord, I understand that.

"But what about my childrens' will?"

Oh! You mean, like, in me?

*"Little one, are you willing
that none should perish?"*

I'd like to say yes, but honesty is best.
There's times I fall short in Your will
Of not being willing that any should perish…

Mercy on the *lost*, and mercy on *me*,
Lord Jesus!

*"The Lord is not slow in keeping his promises, as some understand
slowness. Instead he is patient with you, not wanting anyone to perish,
but everyone to come to repentance."*
(2 Peter 3:9)

*"Who has believed our message, and to whom has the arm of the Lord
been revealed?"*
(Isaiah 53:1)

*"Anyone whose name was not found written in the book of life
was thrown into the lake of fire."*
(Revelation 20:15)

February 2018

From the Rose Flowed Teardrops of Blood

February 2018
Teardrops of blood from the Rose flowed down,
Drenching the stem, then finding the ground,
Forming the river that flows world around,
Teardrops of blood for cleansing.
Many come to the riverbank;
Debate the issue, "truth or prank,"
Thumb their nose, then walk away from the
Ghastly sight they see.
Others come and set up homes, close to the
River they call their own.
Make their living from its wealth, tho'
Set not one foot in it.
Some come seeking soulful peace, trapped
Unfulfilled! Long for release.
So running, dragging, stumbling through,
Until the river comes in view.
They journey on to take the plunge,
Soaking up like human sponge, all the river offers.
All who take the teardrop bath in the river's blood,
Come to understand the truth of the Rose's love
And in eternity's fashion show will be
Purest flowers at the throne;
Praising the Prince of teardrops and blood
The One and Only Rose.

Jesus is the One and Only Rose.
If anything in this poem brings you close to Him,
Then this poem is not in vain.

Forever Blowing

What love is this
That touches me?
From where it comes
I cannot see.
Although I know
The flow of it
To be as simple breeze.
Jesus, I am so thankful
For the gift I could not earn
And do not deserve
But *have*!
Simply because
You are Jesus!
Your grateful servant,
Anthony C. Settles

August 2014

The In-Between

A second before conception transpires,
A second past life expires.
Do you think concerns of any type matter?
Answers accumulate at the in-between.

In those years given you, you're fed
Information from various angles as
From anglers casting for fish.

"Bite my hook, take a look, see the bait,
Eat the bait, investigate, don't be late."
Be sure to swallow hook, line, and sinker
By walking how you will in the in-between.

Who is the man on the boat, giving words
While afloat to those gathered around?
While He, that odd angler,
Cast from boat to dry ground.

What an odd way to fish, hoping to catch
And pull over the water to Him and His boat
With a promise: "In Me, you'll not drown!
But sail beyond the in-between."

Truth Is Absolute

I want to teach what's absolute,
and live an absolute life.
To say it is impossible
is to believe
an absolute lie.
The wanting is the catalyst
to speak an absolute growth,
the knowing is from absolute
as established long ago.
Jesus said, "I am the Way,
The Truth, and the Life."

April 6, 2013

A Poet's Trilogy

See the Boy
Part I

See that boy standing in his grave
He doesn't know how to lie down
He's been shown a book
He took a good look
And now the demons are lookin' his way

And they have fun with his head
In his head they make their bed
Lying tongues, fiery red-hot pokers
Stoking his senses to be evil as theirs
And who cares!

You can't see the tears
Streaming down his face
For they run down the inside
Drenching his soul with mock fulfillment
Emptiness dark and unloving

He stands in his grave, afraid to lie down
Afraid he might drown in the fear of it all
He can't hear the sound of a higher call,
only the voices of his old friends
Who teach him to teach them
That sin is a ball

"Come on," they say
"It will be okay
You're made that way! You're made that way!
You're made that way!"

See the boy stand in his grave
He's his own slave
But who cares?
He's only one boy among millions

A Poet's Trilogy

See the Boy
Part II

Remember that boy
His testimony turned
Time to teach the boy how to climb!
Climb!
Climb!

Chase him demons, pull him down
Kick him, stomp him, call him clown
Tell him all the lies you will
Fill him to the rim with your poison pill
See his hands stretching to the sky
He's tired of believin' your twisted lie

Now whatcha gonna do
When the power is given
Taken that boy from the grave to heaven
Time is a traveler
Traveling forth
It's gettin' time for the angels to rejoice

As the boy lies down in his grave
He is resurrected
Another soul saved.

A Poet's Trilogy

See the Boy
Part III

Now that boy's marching into manhood
Could have been a meltdown
Demons would not stand down
Hope could not let down
For faith to abound
And the demons frowned

They had chased him into puberty
Dragged him through their version of sexuality
Now to burn as they witness
True victory

And prepared to flee
When him they see
Whom they had chased
Now chases he them
A thousand flee
Not by the might of the once-dead boy
But by the truth and the joy
Of the Lord

Spiritual strength for a spiritual race
Fueled by the fire called spiritual grace
Happy to run here and there
Unafraid and blessed to the gospel share

Free in the power of eternal love
Greater is He that is now in the boy
Than he that is in the world
A great chain breaker I know first hand
Freedom is mine
By the Master's plan

1 Corinthians 15:55
"Oh, death where is your sting? Oh, grave where is your victory?"

Color Me, Color Me Not!

Color me whatever you will
Your thoughts cannot change the color I spill
Come the day of recognition
Truth won't hide my definition
Should I stand a lying fool
These colors will come seeping through
Should I stand tried and true?
Colors bright will stick like glue
So color me if you choose
But remember friend whose to lose
For as you paint your picture of me
There's a picture of you being painted
You see.
Thank You, gracious Lord of Hosts
Whose paint brush is the Holy Ghost
I welcome you to color me
With strokes of love pollution-free
In return I'll share the colors
Encouraging all my sisters and brothers.
Flowed bloodred a color one day,
from the Master Painter it did spray
Dare we now judge one another
As though we were a better color?
Color me whatever you will
For the blood of Christ has painted my seal
Hear my plea to you, dear friend
Choose the color that cleanses sin
Once in heaven we can color together
With colors so bright they will fade never!

Crying Softly

Lying awake through early morning hours,
Whispers of truth flooding my soul;
Pressed to cry softly in the shadows of prison
Teardrops to my pillow flow.
For myself the tear drops flow, each crying
out for rain, of the cleansing of His blood
Refresh my soul again.
Slumber comes to those about me, prayers
Spring up to the Father, swell; rejoice in them
I have no problem, for they spring from Father's well.
Crying softly to the rhythm of the teardrops He's placed,
Greater tear drops
Now to offer to my fellow human race.

Words

Only when I see Your face
will I know words worthy of You.
For in this life there are no words
Worthy of what You do.
You never lied while walking
through this world of sinners' nest.
True to Your word, You harbored peace
to all that You have blessed.
I long to speak those worthy words.
I think it won't be long that I will be
speaking worthy words to whom I belong.

Thank you, Jesus, my Savior.

October 2017

Without Your Touch

Without Your touch, who could feel the blowing
winds of change or ride the tides of higher waves
to heights no words can explain?

Demanding an answer is not the answer; that will
stem a desert drought. Rest under the fountain of
His grace and learn who He's all about.

December 2017

Rock the Choir

Gifted voices
Indeed are a treasure
To a listening ear.
A listening ear indeed is a treasure
to a raised voice in need
of an ear to hear.
What a blessing, a "gift to a gift"
Designed to rock the choir!
How dear to the heart
Of the Giver of gifts
Is the sound of a voice
Tho' cracked and hoarse
And the ear in tune
To the sound of rejoice
Be it from the choir
or the cracked and hoarse.
The blessing of gift to gift
Will always rock the choir!

March 11, 2016

Is It Okay?

To live this way
To say these things
To rack my brains
For the things I gain
To cry in pain
Then do it again
Is it okay?
Good question
What does God say?

The Other Man

All through the fall, I saw no love
I looked through my mind and saw no love
Ain't gonna cry 'cause there ain't no love
Love is a dream from another's love

Love put a hand on an empty man
Love took his mind to a higher plan
Crying came in the tears of love
from another man's love it came

Not Make Believe

Romans 10:11

For the scripture does not say
whosoever makes believe
shall not be put to shame.
Tho' all who come to the end of
their game of make believe
will then comprehend the opposite
of you must be born again.
Sad tho' true according to the Word
brought forth of heaven's realm
no one enters by make believe but to believe and leave
shame on the nails!

Not until you come
to the light will
you understand the
opposite of born again,
which in reality is
nothing more than the
sin that lives within!
Bring it to the light,
understand, and repent.
Amen!

Repent

Repent! What does it mean,
Am I bent, perhaps obscene?
Do I fall short of the call?
Am I, to God, too small?
Repent! Is there a way?
Am I too spent, perhaps, to pray?

Do I stand short in the fall?
Am I to God at all?
Repent! It means "to turn";
Yes—you're bent, but not obscene.
And you fall short of the call,
But to God you're not too small.
Repent! There is a way,
You're not too spent, and you can pray.
Of course, you stand short in the fall.
Turn to God. He's *tall*!

Love/Life Learning to Trust

Undefinable,
always climbing to unwind
in the hearts of all who find
themselves intertwined in the vine.
Gives relentless never senseless,
tho' it seems at times, yet in time as we unwind
entangled in the vine,
we find the reasons why.

Meeting New People

Meeting new people
is a blessing with a twist—
First time to see them,
Them to see you.
What a blessing two ways
A gift of His!

Better to Trust in You

Better to trust in You
Than rust outside of you
Step out in faith
And do a thing or two
Obedience is better than sacrifice
Though both are better than rust

Both Roses Dance!

Dance, yellow rose,
Dance while you can.
Dancing days come and go,
So goes the devil's plan.

Red roses love to dance!
In the light of day
Prepared they, "He,"
Eternal bliss, an
Endless dancing stay!

2004

Blossoms of Beauty

Blossoms of Beauty
Bloom in the breeze
Rarest of flowers
Seldom seen
Yet an eye, from
Time to time
Is privileged to behold one
Blossoms of beauty, bloom to
Unfold
Radiant flowers more precious than
gold
The hands of God are theirs
To hold, so graceful
He does clothe them

2004

I Pray
A Prayer in a Jug

I pray He blesses your journey upward, brother
Blessing to the fold; I pray His hands
Forge your feet for flaming walk of soul,
Burn bright, "Now, brother child of light,
And let His will define you!"
I pray your eyes see always clear
His face while on your climb;
In praying His grace to pave the path,
As faith in Him you bind about your heart
In strongest threads, crimson strands of twine.

Nonalcoholic
No Additives|*Only* Preservatives
Ingredients: Loving Prayer for a Friend

2004

I Long

I long, my Lord,
I
You to know.
Your heart in mine,
To grow and grow.
I long, my child,
I
You to know
My heart in Yours,
To grow and grow
And grow and grow
All the way to heaven.

2004

Wolf

I'm aggressive when threatened,
At times, run in packs,
A loner by nature, I cover my tracks.
Trees glide by me as I soar in the race,
Hunt down my food and eat it in place.
I'm not a game player; I know what I am.
In the hands of Creator,
I'm simple and sound!
Seek me and find me wherever you can,
Get not too close, for I'm leery of man.
Admire my sleekness, envy my grace,
Respect if you're wise, my need for my space.
I'm wild, and I'm free,
And at life I don't bluff.
I'm not your pet—

I'm Wolf!

Whose Time

You can spend time
Tho' never really buy time
You can spin time
as tho' it's your time
Will you waste time
on this rhyme
By not hearing what it says?

Colossians 3:17

$ Signs

If dollar signs
are your *ka-ching*
in life,
go study a graveyard
and ask yourself
why.

Pocket

Jesus has a pocket
His pocket has a hole
Nothing ever falls through it
Without a place to go
Every good and perfect gift of His
is truly, fully *whole*.

November 11, 2012

How Awesome

Jesus slept on hay,
Probably not sweet-smelling.
Two thousand years
have come and gone,
still His truth is so worth telling:
Smelly hay to throne of grace.
Being born in every place
where hearts admit unworthy.
How awesome!

December 12, 2012

Always Something

Always something—is it there,
if it's not here,
it's over there,
here and there everywhere.
Something, something I declare,
Is there no end to something!

December 11, 2012

Lie Down, Little Sheep

The Lord came close one cloudy day,
Prepared to wash my rain away.
"Yes!" cried I upon my knees.
"Wash it away if You please."
"Of course, I please," came His reply.
"Lie down, little goat, and die."
So began my walk with my Shepherd,
The rain at times with hail was peppered.
The Lord was there one drowning day,
When I was sinking in the mud;
My Shepherd lifted me out of mud's disgrace
As I pleaded, "Will You, from me, please mud erase?"
"Yes, little lamb, with teardrops and blood,
I'll wash from you the sticky mud."
Now, little sheep, I've helped you grow
And if you want to stay clean,
Lie down at my feet,
For my walk is above all of the old mudholes.

2004

No Cracked Eggs

There will be no cracked eggs in heaven
no one will shop at 7-Eleven
or any other grocery in town, tho' the
storehouse will never shut down
and never in it will ever be found
not even one single cracked egg.
For all of God's eggs are perfected
not salmonella infected, fit to
be broken and rejected, they'll be no
cracked eggs in His town.

Yes! No cracked eggs!
No cracked eggs in heaven.
Tho' they all once were scrambled
over fried and deviled
forget about horses and man
T'was the King who put eggs
back together again
and in heaven there are no
Cracked eggs.

Sea Salt

Grew up not knowin' much about it
Now my home doesn't go without it
Hearty, tasty, friend to my food
Cleansing medicine to my thoughts
And for a side note
Sea salt rocks!

2017

How Long Is the Walk from Point B to Point A?

A stranger took a walk one day,
attempting to reach point B from point A;
causing confusion along the way seemed the destination.
Crap! cried the stranger of the messy path,
"everywhere I step,"
Oh well! You do the math.

What is this stranger saying?
What is this stranger steppin' in?
In the path along the way to point B from point A
and exactly what is the point of point B and point A?
And what makes the stranger a stranger?
And is it all a hopeless mess?
Take a guess, do your best,
perhaps you'll solve the puzzle.
Drop the muzzle and proclaim
His grace
through the length of the walk
from point B to point A.

December 23, 2017

How Beautiful the Feet

How much money would you
spend on your feet?
Should investment value add
comfort to your travel?

Shoes of all sizes, makes, and models,
adding up to many dollars,
all for the purpose of treating them kind.

Those two things we call dogs
that love to bark when they're
tired and achy, and let's not
forget bunions, corns, hammertoes,
the ouch of flat feet
hurting two-fold; so off we go
traveling through life while
treating our feet.

Romans 10:15 NKJ
"As it is written, 'How beautiful
are the feet of those who preach
the gospel of peace,
who bring glad tidings of good things.'"

Christian feet may march
till they bleed, once filled with
the depth of His love while
understanding the beauty they carry,
worth more than all measure of blood!

How beautiful the feet.

July 16, 2018

One Hot Day

While mowing the yard
between church times,
I felt unusually queasy
in my kneezy.
Oh, pleazy don't make
fun of my choice of words.
The dusty made me sneezy,
and the water dripped off me
like crazy; the whole ordeal
made me feel lazy and hazy.
It was even a chore to pick up little sticks,
and then the true problem came to light
the heat index was 106º.
The end.

Solve the problem:
2 Timothy 2:15

2018

Pick

Pickin' the nose is a baby's means
of explorin' a part of a place unseen—
that is, to the baby, nose-pickin'!

All else can see up the little one's nose—
except the owner of that very same nose
who also happens to be you, see.
The very same one
you see who picks
at his own little toes.

So that nose-pickin', toes-pickin'
little bundle of joy,
shouts out to the world or as much as it knows:
"I'm unashamed of my nose
or my toes, I just got to know,
What…do…they mean? Why are they
there, if not for pickin'? I don't
have a clue."

Untaught they'll cling
to pickin' well beyond the time of being cute.

Enjoy and train those to the world you bring,
and be blessed in the doing of it.

As you guide them to be true
to their nose and those toes
and all the in-between.

2017

Tiny Tony's Testimony: Mumble, Mumble Bumble Bee

Mumble, mumble bumble bee,
Where's my maw? I gotta pee;
off to the outhouse we did go,
a'takin' care of business.
One step, two steps, three steps,
four, makin' our way to
the outhouse door.
Complicated it could be,
without Maw 'cause I was only three.
Open door and step inside;
down my legs my trousers slide;
set me up on outhouse throne.
Mama did with arms quite strong,
letting go just long enough
and turn around the door to shut.
Shutting door, an easy thing,
should not cause a Tony scream.
Whirled back around, my head
to see disappear beneath
the toilet seat.
Mumble, mumble, bumble bee,
Where's my maw? I'm in the pee
And other unmentionables.
Mother reached as far as she could,
stretched to save her son,
Which I am most thankful for.
She thought nothing of her own dilemma.
Twenty years later, on a trailer floor

in Ronan, Montana,
I felt as far as God was concerned,
I was forever in eternity's outhouse—
An outhouse incomparable and
far worse than the one my
mother, bless her heart,
pulled me out of.
God's arm is not short; it
can reach to the farthest places,
and He will reach to a
crying heart regardless of
where it's crying from.
If it's crying for Him,
He is awesome and full of grace.

Does It Make a Noise

Let me be one
who has an ear to hear
words of truth, in this
forest of falling trees
all about me, that these
lies that surround me, pleading
to come back into me,
have no choice but to
leave me, when I do not
hear the noise of the falling
trees in the forest
because my ears are in
You, Lord, Your Word
is awesome!

October 15, 2018

Where Be My Pencil?

Where be my pencil?
I haven't a clue
I guess this old ink
pen will just have to do.

Has anyone seen that
pencil of mine?
I guess when I left
I just left it behind.

Oh! For an eraser to
erase what I write
then fill in the
smudge marks
with more writing delight.

Oh, that my writings
where marbled in stencil
then would I stick
to the use of the pencil?

Till I find my pencil
I know without doubt
I'll find plenty of
use for the gift of Wite-Out.

And should typing
even come in to play
for me and my
headache
please pray!

Jonah and the Smelly Belly

Trapped inside
the dark and gloomy,
if I'll live—I cannot tell.

One thing I'm sure,
my nose is certain
I'm trapped within
an awful smell.

No running from it,
no place to go,
the stench seems immersed
in the depth of my soul.

Tho' I cry,
Will God ever hear me?
So bad is the smell.
can He even be near me?

I wonder in silence
as I ponder my plight:
Is this how I smell to God
when I disobey light?

Mercy, Lord, tho' I am smelly,
deliver me from this
old dark belly,
and I'll go where I'm told.

May you mold me like jelly,
just get me out of this ole
smelly belly.

While Sweeping the Floor

While sweeping the floor
in a slow work day,
it came over me to worship
and pray.
"Can I worship You as I sweep
the floor?" I said as I swept
to the tune of my Lord.
His voice touched my soul in
instant reply, "Worship away.
Yes, worship awhile,"
and I did, and it was great;
made sweeping a joy in the
midst of the dust. Yes, I say
in the midst of the dust,
I swept away.
What joy, what joy.
Amen!

Sweet Sadness

Sweet sadness, how can it be? Is sadness ever a pleasure?
Oh, but, dear friend, there can come a time
when sadness can be such a treasure.
Times of sadness most unique, laid wide open at His feet;
I speak of Spirit's inspired sadness.
A longing heart to quench the fire, brought about by soul's desire,
For a closer walk with God, the prompter of sweet sadness.
Sadness gracing quiet joy, peaceful sadness is the story
Of a broken heart that aches, bending gently till it breaks
Into a closer walk of day.

Sweet sadness, such an instrument played by the meek, *of Him*
Who offers the brightest fellowship by turning off the dim.
Oh, yes! Dear friend, sweet sadness times will come,
And as you grow, you'll recognize the harmony they strum;
And rejoice at the chance to fall deeper in love with the
Author of sweet sadness.

If this poem helps one heart
that has touched the sadness
I speak of, then this poem
has not been in vain.

Treasures of the Trees

Trees blown by the breeze,
leaves wave praises,
to the One who sees
all the richness implanted in a tiny little seed.
Height to the climber,
heat to the cold,
planks for housing, food for the fold,
trees a gift of value untold;
most worthy of reflection.
Consider how birds nest in their heights,
animals hug them on cold wintry nights,
clothed with snow, what a marvelous sight
are trees.
Hidden splendor in disguise,
from limb to splinter, spring surprise.
Their Designer sure is wise
to formulate the trees.
Can any count the many times you've
met our endless needs?
Is there a way to calculate the depths
within Your seeds?
Yes! The air is truly blessed at your
very sneeze, and the ground is fertilized;
come time for you to cease,
and in all that's known,
we're yet to touch
the treasure of the trees.

1998

Lie Down, Rag Doll

Lie down, Rag Doll.
You are so sweet,
Said the little girl
With the doll at her feet.
Rag Doll lay with loveless eyes—
Only a rag doll, no surprise.
Yet her love for the rag doll fell
Over the doll in a loving veil,
Much like Rag Doll people are.
Tho' His love is never far
At His feet, lie we down,
Rag dolls dressed in human gown.
Unlike Rag Doll's handmade eyes,
To ours can come such sweet surprise
Love from the hand that made us so
Can flood the eyes of a rag doll soul.

Before 2006

Not a Head Cloud

When Jesus spoke of eternity,
He was not speaking metaphorically
of sweet dreams placed in your head
for the purpose of comfort until you're dead.

The dead will rise *(1 Thessalonians 4:16)*,
heads with eyes will see the truth
without disguise.

To many, a sweet blessing,
sadly to most, most depressing
(Matthew 7:13).
Truth in love came to me one day,
though I had heard it many times.
Truth in love (in a special way),
so I turned from sin; it came to stay.

Have you turned from sin to follow Him,
Whose love awaits us all *(John 3:16)*?
Truth in love now bleeds through His,
Let Him save you from the fall! *(Romans 3:23)*

John 14:6 says:
"Jesus said to him,
I am the way, the truth,
and the life, no one comes
to the Father
except through Me."

June 12, 2015

Gave His All

Gave His all, for all that fall,
all that fall already fell.

How is it so, how can it be,
that all who fall, already fell?

Deeper ground is what we need
to touch the sower of the seed.

Plant your feet now to the ground,
grab the plow, but don't look down.

Up and onward you must plow
In love with your Redeemer.

December 13, 2012

Jezebel's Bones

Who sent the dogs to lick Jezebel's bones?
That fly on the wall,
that stench of death
masquerading in the land
as a woman of wealth.

Did she not know that
crippled people cannot outrun
fleet-footed dogs
that are destined to come?
And come they did when the time was right,
to lick the bones
without the fight,
of this unrepentant sinner.
Oh, Jezebel, it was foretold:
1 Kings 21:23

Long before it was your time
your flesh, the dogs to feed.
What could have you done?
What should you have done?
Now what did you do, Jezebel?

You could have heeded
the word foretold,
you should have relented
hardness of soul;
you chose, however, to
let it grow

into that blood-splattered mess on the wall,
bringing the foretold dogs
that God sent.

All of life has a foretold telling
of what's to come in the proper time.

For all who choose not to believe
the account of Jezebel,
let me refer you to
2 Timothy 3:16.

For all who believe it's a fairy tale,
let me refer you to
the woman at the well
John 4:29.

For all who think nothing of it at all,
let me refer you to the grave,
and ask yourself,
"What awaits my bones?"

You are referred to
John 5:28–29.

Wow!

For every thought known to man,
None can claim to be so grand.
As a thought that followed through,
In love with them who follow.
Follow me, said He who had no sin,
I'll take you to a place where thoughts
Cannot erase the meaning of my grace;
So solid is that place you'll know me
Face to face and taste in full
The beauty of love without flaw.
No more mirrors of iniquity, nor reflection of
Wanna be. All will be as sound as me, you see.
I thought it long ago and soon you're gonna know
In full. For now just give thanks and claim wow!

2017

He Has Decided

He has decided to take those to heaven
who simply follow Him—
an irrevocable promise given only to them.
He has decided!

With a promise to any who call on His name,
that they too can come and be one
and the same as those who follow Him.
He has decided!

And remember, dear brother and sister in Christ,
separation from His presence is forever dying
with no ending in sight.
He has decided!

So station yourselves, you soldiers of faith,
in this battlefield of life.
Study your bibles, work your sword,
and pray God to grant new life.
He has decided!

April 2018

Spot

Dark spot from the distant *son*,
a blemish in the universe had begun.

Hide little spot as well as you can,
His eyes of truth will spot your plan,
to be a truth as truth is.

Never His plan to dim a light,
but to light the night
you can't use a black light.

Come little dot
now to the right spot
where the *right light* can bless you.

November 2017

King Over Pain

Welcomed are those
who have means to obtain
the absence of pain
to the structured frames
of all who live and die.
For
pain has no friends,
no sense of shame
to the flavor it brings
of racked up pain
for the structured frames
of all who live and die.
So
who would welcome
such suffered guest,
let alone request on the
birthday list as invite to the party
for all who live and die?
He
who so loved the world
embraced it all!
Including all pain brought
by the fall
of all who live and die!
JOHN 3:16

December 16, 2017

Hear Ye, Hear Ye

Hear ye, hear ye,
children of the Lord
I've questions to ask
and plead they not be ignored.

Is it arrogant to
know Jesus and to know
how to know Him?
Is it arrogant to
stand in the gap and
reveal what's bestowed Him?

The world would have
you silenced of Jesus—
the one and only.
To then sell the goods
of all varied connections
declaring arrogant
all who don't buy them!

Stand fast, don't fall.
Let Jesus stand tall
after all, it's He who
purchased the market;
now with a loving heart
speak truth to the blind
as His light shines to the
path that
humbles the arrogant.

June 2018

Draw Me Nigh

Draw my heart nigh unto you, Lord.
If it has to bleed,
please don't let it die.
For mercy's sake, I plead my case
for you to draw me nigh.
Enemies around me
surround me with lies.
I've sinned enough of my own,
I'm unable to disguise
before Your all-seeing eyes,
all the truth of me,
so mercy is my plea.
Let every man be a liar,
but you, Lord, are true.
I'm pleading for your mercy
and trusting it to you.
Draw me nigh, Lord.
Draw me nigh!

August 2018

When! Where! How!

When loud is always peaceful,
And quiet is never followed by a raging storm,

Where the sound of silence speaks
Volumes and high-decibel noise calms souls,

As praises from both intermix in a
Chorus put together by heavenly host,
Which brings us to the how—

How can quiet be heard with no need to strain an ear?
How can the eardrum not burst at the loud so near?

Balance of the inner ear—could that be the answer?
Volume control designed
by the hand of the Master.

In tune, in pitch, in perfect harmony.
The quiet of noise stirs the silence from
Loud to the ear controlled by the hearing
Aid of the Father;

As the loud in the quiet can crank high
and lofty with batteries kept charged
simply at the cost of prayer.

How you ask and what more is there,
Obedience to the doctor of your head,
not your own head, is key for all to
understand how quiet and noise can blend.

Now is the when, you are the where, and
How is from the doctor of your head.

Maker of forever!

March 14, 2015

Sweet Relief

Sailing through this world
one very hot day
with no shade in sight,
a breeze blew into the
sweat of my face
and, oh, what a sweet relief.

The breeze left
but the heat stayed,
still no shade
while the sweat poured,
but thoughts of the
breeze filled my sails
with hope for
the sweet relief.

Sail on, sailor,
there's more heat to come.
Shadeless days,
and sweat drops
big as plums,
much like the
ones Jesus shed,
bidding you to anchor down
on Sunday morning.

Refresh your sails
for the journey around.
Oh, what sweet relief!
Thank You, Jesus. Amen!

September 2018

Boom! God *Is* Good

Not a little white lie, not even a tiny one;
put all the Bible says under a microscope
and try to find a trace of little white lie;
so prompts the devil to the unregenerate mind.
While they consider the Bible,
he points out the whys "of hath God said"
twisting all he can to fit his ultimate plan of painting
a picture of himself as an angel of light;
no surprise at his white lie disguise,
as he is the father of them!
Blinding their eyes, they go about teaching
lies for truth with smiles on their faces,
filling the ditch of the blind turning His Holy Book
into a book full of holes undefined.
Not only a little white lie, not even a hint of truth,
under the microscope take a look there's plenty of
visible proof that the Bible has no trace of truth, so
prompts the devil to unregenerate minds as they marvel
at the clockwork of space and time.
Their views of scripture rust in the field of nonsense,
as they trust their intelligence to the clockwork
unwind, and make sense of the clockwork's precision,
attempting to throw His Holy Book into a world full of
holes to be lost forever, and be rid of all
thoughts of divine!
Not a bold dark lie, nor a whitewashed devil can keep
a sinner from heaven. Believe the truth and be set free.

Come to know you're in sync with the Savior.
He loves you, and in Him you'll find no lie.
Boom, God is good!

Read Luke 13:27, 2 Timothy 3:16–17

October 2018

Twisted Twister

From darkened clouds, comes twisting down
A twister of destruction, upon our states it
devastates, leaving souls for broken, cry
in the wind, deny the sin, it's you the winds
are choking, it's party time, it's party
time have a beer drink some wine
roll a joint, smoke some coke
and dare not judge another!
After all we're all in all one
big party—brother—should
by chance you get bound
up by a slight addiction,
worry not for a program will
deal with your affliction.
Higher power is okay, choose
one to your liking, pull
it out when you feel
down, and drink the
juice it's spiking.
If this country
doesn't turn
back to the
Blesser of its
shores, He
will not
forbid the
twister
twist
till this
country
is no
more.

Birthday Touch Times Two

There is a touch
that sparks a flame
enabling two to harvest gain.
What is the gain you want to know?
Look in your mirror and let it show—
You are the gain—happy birthday!

You were the gain to His creation,
Male and female, He created them.
The apple of His eye is who you are.
Let no one tell you different—happy birthday!
Understand there is a touch
of a past and a future time.

Sparking flames,
enabling three to harvest gain.
Born again, gain more precious
than a pure golden apple,
because you are the apple
of His eye!

Happy birthday!

2018

Apple

Shiny apple in my hand,
I take a bite,
the juice runs down my chin,
I wipe it off, and take another bite;
"so sweet within,"
is it a sin
to bite into the apple? The answer's no, as apples go;
God made them to His pleasure, scrumptious fruit, to my taste,
to me a pallet treasure; so eat my fill, unreel the peel,
or leave it in the wrapper; it matters not to this ole boy, "I
love to eat my apple." Shiny apple, beneath your skin
much more than meat to plunder;
for your core, that inner sore is not of
Godly blunder, what bitter taste,
I thought such waste, until my eyes were opened
to a timely insight
of why the core was spoken.

Shiny apple on your tree, God created you and me; from the tree,
into my hand, God's Begotten laid a plan; as I thank Him for
your sweetness, I'm reminded of my weakness
within your walls, of pleasant taste
resides a bitter nesting place; where seeds
wade through the rotting pace;
find the ground and die to self; to live again a
tree of wealth. Shiny apples to God's eye,
are we humans earthly grown; let's thank Him for analogies of
what our seeds have sown; within us, is bitterness, blooming
from conception; sins of lies, that lead to cries eternal in deception.

Shiny apples, to the Son, are all the souls of life
begun, as our inner core gives way, seeds of God find
ground to pray, growing upward in His grace;
Trees of life sway in His face, "Praising apples,"
shining bright to the giver of the light.
One shiny apple stood the test, who's core was never "sinfulness";
hanged, bruised, and fed to worms; upon His tree He hung,
I ask Him, apple of the ages, why allowed You
to be tortured? For you He said and all the rest
of Father's apple orchard. Shiny apple in my heart,
I pray your juice run through me
forbid my hand, to wipe away the cleansing of its beauty
that when I lay before Your throne perfectly
unblemished, praising You I'll be ripe through,
from skin to core, plum finished.

If any, gain any insight to the wisdom of God from
this poem, then this poem has not been in vain.

2003

Caring Hand

In Honor of Craig and Jana Reaves

It is always special
When loved ones show
A caring hand in times of
Uncertainty

I know of two who take to heart
The caring hand you chose to stretch
It touched the two
With warmth and a smile
And we two are very grateful

Rock Away, Baby

Mother sits in the midnight air
Rocking baby from the rocking chair
Baby's safe in Mama's care
Rock away, baby, rock away
Rock away, baby, rock away!

Mother cuddles her baby soft
Lays baby down in a cradle loft
Baby's sleep is sweet and oft
Rock away, baby, rock away
Rock away, baby, rock away!

Baby comes and baby grows
Proven fact that Mama knows
Off to the chair again she goes
Baby in the arms of loving flow
Rock away, baby, rock away
Rock away, baby, rock away!

1998

Watch the Hat

Taiya's HS Graduation

Long time coming,
but there it goes,
hat flying through the air.

Lots of hard work, some fun,
fellowship, and knowledge gained
of many things,
attached to that flying hat.

How awesome
that the benefits to the
hat are left in the head.

Now go get 'em,
you graduate, and
congrats
for a job well done.

It is Good to Grow

To watch someone grow
is a blessing defined by
the eyes of those who
do the watching.

To grow is defined in
the eyes of the ultimate
Watcher.

We have been privileged
to watch you grow into
who you are!

And we love who we see.

Remember that it is good
to grow first and foremost
spiritually!

"Mentally and emotionally
will always follow suit."

Congratulations

Not just for graduating
but first and foremost
being you!

Keep growing because

It is good to grow!

Remee Prayed

Of all you left behind
A legacy of prayer
A husband who will miss you
Children who love to kiss you
Friends who want to be like you
In the way your life inspires.

Of all you left behind
Troubled hearts mended
At the prayers you prayed
Tears of joy replacing
Tears of pain and grief.

Of all you left behind
Relief to the missionary time and again
Release to the prisoner trapped in sin
A lot of hallelujahs and a ton of amens
Flowing through the fold of us
From the prayers of your prompting
Sister Remee!

Of all you left behind
To all the loves of Remee's life
When you feel you're stuck in reverse
You want to want to move forward
But can't seem to shift gear
And out of the blue the transmission is loosed
And forward you're moving with ease
Remember, Remee prayed.

People come and people go
Their legacies remain
When prayer life is your legacy
Prayers answered will proclaim
Of all the blessings you have left
none more powerful
Than Remee prayed.

July 31, 2016

Come Learn from Me

In Memory of David Daniels

Such wonderful words
To the student of joy
Beginning at Class 101.
Repentance unto salvation,
Graduating at the end
With the degree of
"O grave, where is thy victory,
death where is thy sting?"
only in Him.

Will you go learn from Him
as Mr. David did?
Rewards are promised
not to someone dead,
But rather to life alive and
life well lived.
Faithful and true to the
One who said,
"Hey, David,
Come learn from me"
And David answered the call.

That Mr. David,
Carburetor man by trade,
Christian man by grace
Through faith in Christ, his Lord.

Some might think of him
Unpaid for devotion to the
Work of his hands
As he mowed church grass,
Blessing the view of many
Whom he never knew,
Or loving on his grands,
Blessing them in many ways—
Though they yet to fully understand.

Oh, that student of joy, Mr. David,
who loved singing a song and telling a joke!
"They'll be shouting
On the hills of glory"
Has turned into this:

"*There is* shouting on the
Hills of glory" and
Rewards past tense
Lying at the foot of Him
Who said,
"Hey, David, come learn from me."

March 2017

Holding Sue's Hand

"I am so tired and ready to go,
so I'll see you on the other side, my good friend"
were the last words Miss Sue spoke to me.
And tho' my visits were a few more,
no more words came my way,
only the sound of tired sleep from a worn-out frame
whose hand I was honored to hold.
It all began—that is, the holding of her hand—
with an invite for a visit to her house.
Such a sweet offer to a soon-to-be-wed couple.
We accepted with joy and looked forward
to our time with Miss Sue,
perhaps have some tea or freshly brewed coffee
while sitting down to some friendly chat
in sweet fellowship, spawning gentle waves
of light laughter ending with hugs at the door!
Now a question for all of you:
does that sound a bit syrupy sweet?
Well, let me repeat the part about hugs at the door
As that part came to pass,
not so much on the syrupy sweet:
"Quit your smoking, it's no joke, don't be a doofus.
You're getting married!"
Short on syrup but long on love
was my introduction to the heart of Miss Sue
whose hand I was privileged to hold.
Held it I did from time to time
at the end of each visit while praying to Father
after having our talks of the whatevers of life,
rolling our eyes at each other at times,
reminding each other that life

is a rhyme that often shows no reason—
and apart from faith in the Master's hand.
It only grows cold at the end of its season,
and we would hold hands and pray.
The Master's hand holds all of His
and He's given us all hands to hold
to help and to fold filled with faith
at the end of this journey.
One of mine was my dear sister, Sue.
I hope to have many more,
and hope for some to hold my hand
at the time of death's revolving door
whose entrance is dark, and exit is light
to the glory of the Lord.
Thank you, Jesus, the only conqueror over death
for holding Sue's hand
not only to, but altogether through the door.

August 26, 2018

Excited to Exist

Abortion was no vision
in the eyes of a mother's wisdom;
conception gave her reason
to embrace her growing womb,
and in nature's time to
bloom forth a yellow
wrinkled flower with
hair long and jaundice strong.
Bringing pain to the
flower bed, my mother.
Mother's pain subsided
shortly after I ignited
the delightful flow of
love a mother knows.
And tho' it's far from perfect
in this fallen world
we're born in, I'm thankful
that my mother saw the value
of her little thorny rose!

Mothers, whatever circumstance
brings about conception,
please understand there is
a master plan. Now may truth
in love direct you to
comprehend that your life is
no more valuable than
any other—so have your baby
and learn of a mother's love
to experience their
excitement to exist!

February 2, 2016

Lay Down the Law

Laid down the law
did the man to his family,
"My way or the highway,"
said he with a smirk. Then opened the door
in the heart of this daddy of a law laid down,
nailed to the ground
in the hands and feet
of redemption.
Propitiation to abound
where grace in the daddy
now is found,
filling his heart with love.
To then lay down the laws
he had to his family, laid down,
picking up God's law of love
instead of selfish delusion.

2013

He Was Not a Turkey Roosting in a Tree

More than a turkey bird,
more than green beans,
gravy, potatoes, stuffing, yams
beside juicy slices of ham,
and not to forget,
pecans, punkin', and sweet tata pie,
oh my, my
oh my, my slap myself silly,
make one wanna cry.
I'm plum stuffed like a goose.
How will I lose
my extra caboose? Oh, well
'twas a worthy cause.
People and friendships,
family and friends,
strangers I might never see again, opportunity
reminding me once a year
that truth is more than vittles to eat,
but year around, moment by moment, smorgasbord complete.

Matthew 22:37
Love the Lord Your God
with all your Heart, Soul and Mind;

John 13:34
Love One another
as I have loved you;

Matthew 19:19
Love your neighbor
as yourself;

Matthew 5:44
Love your enemies;

And be thankful always
for He has done
great and mighty things.

"For You see
He was not a Turkey
Roosting in a tree,
But God on a Tree
Dying for You and Me"

November 28, 2015

More Stuffed Than the Turkey!

More stuffed than the turkey
are those who feast
from the Father's throne.
More plump than the goose
are those who feast:
a buffet of living food and drink
to all who come and feast.
The more you eat
the healthier your soul.
There's no eating too much; take your fill,
more stuffed than the turkey
is Father's will.
More plump than the goose.
Please Him so,
don't slow down.
Eat some more,
table always full
and our Host offers more
for stuffing you is
His lingering joy!

November 27, 2016

A Basket of Bread to the Christian Head

Would you walk through life with a basket of bread—
A basket of bread on your head,
Passing out bread as you go through life
in hopes of feeding the dead.
Filling the basket with His word, keeping it filled to the top
While knowing the load gets no lighter as
long as the filling doesn't stop.

Pass it out, fill it up, keep it weighted down.
Will you go through life, my friend, passing the bread around?
Jesus is the Bread of Life the world can all afford.
He's never been out of stock, though often goes ignored.
Snack foods are a supplement; fast food may be a detriment.
Junk foods are experiments sent to tempt your taste buds sore.
Jesus is pure health food with redeeming power to cure.

So remember where you come from, for once you had no bread.
You gained it from a basket on another brother's head.
Again I ask the question: "How will you walk through life?"
Pleasing the crowds of starvation or bearing true Bread of Life.

2005

Stable

It was a dark and dreary stable in a cubby hole
Where Christ child drew first breath.
Many times I'd heard the tale of One laid in a manger,
Yet to me, I must confess, He was a foreign stranger.
Who was He to such as me, a man who'd shunned His table?
Then came the day I recognized my life a dreary stable.
My mind went to the words I'd heard of much more than a child.
I thought of how He'd grown and died for sinners tame or wild.
It hurt to look within myself, for there dwelt beast of burden.
I pondered, could there be some truth to
Christ whom I'd been learning
To my stable door come knocking! Should I open up?
I made my choice to not regret, and guess who comes to sup?
Jesus still comes to be born in darkest dreary stable,
now with joy I spread the Word; I know He's not a fable.
Is your life confused, my friend? Are you cold and lonely?
Take another look and find Christ's birthplace now is empty!
He moved away to higher realm; though He still is seeking
places to be born, dear friend,
stables for His keeping.

Christmas Afterthought

When it's all said and done,
When all toys are put away
From the first day of play;
When leftovers are frozen
in freezer bag display;
And you lay your head in rest,
will you be one of the
very, very blessed
with an understanding?
So few have.
Amidst the shoving just
to grab a gift before another can, to score a
prize from Santa Claus!
Will you be able to lay
your head in beautiful rest,
having focused in truth
on the humble little nest
where lay Baby Jesus?

November 26, 2014

Merry Christmas Poem!

In the gift of poetry
often read to tell a story
as unchangeable and timeless
as history's unfolding mysteries,
how can it be done in
short Christmas verse?
Simple now, be blessed
in one word

A name—Jesus!

December 25, 2014

A Short Christmas Devotion

In the belief that a short Christmas devotion on a pre-Christmas day
Means more to You, Jesus, than all the sanctimonious array,
We humbly come to You. We humbly raise our hands to You
With our hearts held loosely in them,
offering them to You in devotion.
Will You once again take our hearts from
our hands and hold them in Yours?
Energize them with love, make them sound,
soft and pliable in the image of Yours
So that we do not fall short of loving one another and all
Others this coming year.
Examine our hearts and bless our devotion to Your good pleasure
So that we can, in obedience to You, forgive the offenders,
Love all pretenders
In hopes of surrender to someday perhaps.
Have this short Christmas devotion on a pre-Christmas day,
Meaning more to You than all sanctimonious array!
To You we come devoted. Thank You, Jesus!

December 2015

Candle Snuffer

Candle begins with a *C*,
as does Christ our Lord.
Snuffer starts with an *S*,
as does Satan for sure.

Candle snuffer, will you
snuff us candles if you can?
Snuffing us is snuffing light,
not our Maker's plan!

Now you see me,
now you don't:
A game of hide and seek
under his unwashed
water of lies—snuff
goes the candle.

Destroying fire whose
flames stretch high
to lengthen the darkest night:
called by your name
the wicked one,
evil angel of light—and
snuff goes the candle.

Two cars in your garage,
a chicken in every pot.
Focus on the haves you have
while crying over the nots.
Don't stop there and do declare
It's all about the blessing.
What is that frizzled
hissing? *Snuff*
goes the candle.

He's a student of purpose
who hunts down the candles,
not wasting time on
those he can't snuff:
obedient candles,
not falling for fluff
or stuff or foolish bluff—
bright burns the candle.

September 2013

Candle's Wax

Every drop is important
In the candlemaker's shop.
You'll never find Him cleaning up
with an ordinary mop.

Hot sponges with holes
to sip and sop
'til wax is set for perfect drop
and then one final stop.
Refurbishing His
candle!

Flicker to Flame

Flicker to flame,
no shame in fire,
curling up smoke,
dissipating in time.
A candle's rhyme
and reason;
a candle stuck
without a cure
for the melting wax
that's less than pure
has one choice that
will not fail. Simple
to the common
candle, costly to the
most mishandled.
How does the candle
plea? Is there shame
in the smoke?
Take hope, take hold,
candles of this
candelabrum;
smoke of a holy fire
is a gift of grace of
His desire!
Reaching the candle
maker sweet incense
to His breathing. He
exhales on your
pleading.
Mercy to the
bleeding candle wax.

October 2013

Candle's Tear Drop

Rains came,
candles kept flame,
winds blew,
some flames grew.
Floods, famines, quakes,
and pestilence
beat the candle.
Mysterious are all
who live in the dark
to deflame the candles.

Yet on the hills,
the candles start
in candlestands of His holy plan.
At times so bright,
the world has no choice
but to see them.
Other times so dim,
a teardrop could extinguish them.
Yet how is it that
tear drops feed them?

Come to the place
called Teardrop Springs.
Its water to the candles is kerosene.

Come, learn the history of
the hill where a candle stood—
as all alone
to the eyes that watched
at the foot of the hill.

Come, learn the splendor
of the flame that bled bright red,
Though the candle was broken and tired.

Come, learn how the flame went on to expire,
or so thought those at the foot of the hill.

Until the flame rekindled;
Hallelujah in the glow!
Brighten the story in the teardrop's flow.

On the hill there are lights,
burning lights giving light to the night.
Where is yours? Is it bright?
Is it fed in the flow? Have you grown?
Does your flame burn a joyous amen
that let His glories transcend
to all at the foot of the Hill?

November 2013

Candle Book

"Wow! What is that book on the table, Master Candlemaker?" "Come now and see, for I am so glad you asked, little candle that I made in the likeness of me. It's time to open it up for you to have a look, but be careful not to damage your wick with a lick of flame from the book until it's time for you to take your place on your page in my book."

"Wow! That'll preach," said Little Candle as Master Candlemaker grinned at him, setting Little Candle's flame aglow. "I know," said Little Candle, "the book's not yet for show, only tell." Little Candle grinned at himself at his clever dialogue with Master Candlemaker.

Blinded by the light at first glance, Little Candle sensed the wicked at the core of his wick and started to pray he could just melt away.

And then, just as Master Candlemaker promised, the intensity subsided and His shield surrounded and then provided the perfect peephole for Little Candle. But, oh, what a show there was to see! The candles stood still but their flames were on fire in a holy dance of Master's desire. No rhythm could keep up, no rhyme was given to greet and inspire; He who put dance in the fire and Little Candle shook at want for the life of the book, splattering wax on Master

Candlemaker who promptly molded it into
a new name given and then sealed with His
own wax onto Little Candle's own page in
Master Candlemaker's book.

My friends, can you consider yourselves the
Little Candle in this poem? Is your name in the book?

December 2013

Candelabrum Seven

I am so imperfect.
My hand, so weak.
Pen unclear as to the
seven I speak about.
Yet compelled am I
to finish the quest:
Candelabrum Seven.

My mind will not
shut off.
Things that usually
occupy
pass by
unmeaningfully.

Candelabrum Seven is in my vision,
and I stretch to see the light
more bright than these eyes can handle.
Sunglasses unwelcomed to the task I take
for the light would only melt them.
And I yearn for His candle to burn within me—
Perfect is He who burns bright
in the lives of those He's taking.

Strong is His hand
and His pen so clean
as He rewrites the lives of His making.
Beauty in the light, always His delight,
regardless that we are unworthy.

Soon enough more than see—
in Him, I am and will always be
Candelabrum Seven.

Candelabrum
represents heaven;
Seven
equals perfection.

February 2014

His Journey

From a baby to a man
He lived to love
From a Man to the cross
He showed who He was
From the cross to the crown
who He was He still is
Eternal Redeemer to all of His kids

December 21, 2012

About the Author

There is an old gospel song titled "God Leads Us Along." The chorus goes, "Some through the waters, some through the flood, some through the fire, but all through the blood, some through great sorrow, but God gives a song in the night season and all the day long."

Anthony C. Settles's life from early on was peppered with gospel truth; however, the salt did not arrive until the age of twenty-three when he confessed his sins—which were many—to God. From his trailer floor in Ronan, Montana, two thousand miles from where he grew up and two thousand years after the crucifixion, death, and resurrection of the man called Jesus, by His grace, Anthony took his Dutch-Irish-Cherokee-English hillbilly self to the foot of the cross, and there discovered that Jesus had already discovered him, knew him like a book, and bade him look in His book while saving his soul despite the rebellious man he has become.

He has since spent time as a rescue mission worker, jail minister and worker, and cross-country traveler. He is a preacher, poet, and now at sixty-two, a seafood monger.

He lives in Beaufort, South Carolina, where he met and married his tenacious wife, Paula, who blesses him immeasurably. Her mom, Polly, has come to live with them and she adds to the blessing of their home. Their lives are enriched with church, fellowship, and ministry.